I WANT TO BE A SOCIAL MEDIA MARKETER

Written by
Vivek Ramachandran

Edited by
Jonathan Reule

Illustration
Chong Wey Ming

Copyright © 2022 by Unibino Pte. Ltd.

All rights reserved. No part of this publication may be reproduced, stored in a retrieval system, or transmitted, in any form, or by any means, electrical, mechanical, photocopying, recording or otherwise without the prior written permission of the publisher or a licence permitting restricted copying.

First paperback edition November 2022
ISBN 978-981-18-6071-3

Published by Unibino Pte. Ltd.
31 Rochester Drive Level 3, #03-47 Singapore 138637

www.unibino.com

Communication has always been important for animals and humans alike. Dogs bark when excited, cats meow when hungry, birds chip and sing at the break of dawn, while elephants trumpet loudly to say hello. But humans have taken this form of communication beyond simple sounds and utterances to the point of forming their own unique languages that have empowered us over time.

Ah Gah Ah Gah!!
With such advanced language abilities, humans were better able to work together, build tools for protection against larger animals, and execute complex plans as a team.
?!
Nok Nok!
Hok Hok?

This led to the eventual exchange of ideas, mutual collaborations, and great inventions that would change the course of mankind's history.

From then on, humans found various methods to share their ideas and communicate with one another. With cave paintings, carving words into blocks of stone, and even writing on early forms of paper, known as papyrus.

In time written information became more readily available all over the world after the printing press was created. More books were printed, and more people were able to learn simply by reading, which gave mankind's communication a big boost.

For several hundreds of years, books were the main source of written information. That is until the computer came along. After its arrival, we were able to store vast amounts of data and written information on them while saving space and keeping our files well organised for easy retrieval.

But in 1989, our communicative abilities took another giant leap forward when Tim Berners-Lee invented the internet! It allowed computers to connect all over the globe, giving us the chance to talk with almost anyone, no matter the distance.

Google

As the internet evolved, websites offered a seemingly infinite amount of knowledge, more than a million books worth! And with search engines like Google, finding that information could be accomplished in a matter of seconds. Best yet, Email gave us a way to communicate with our family and friends for free, no matter how far away, and at a much faster rate than typical snail mail.

Although, with everything the internet had, it was still missing relationships and shared experiences that only the real world could offer at that time.

That is until social media websites were created. With platforms such as Facebook, Instagram and Twitter, people were able to remain connected to their loved ones and share experiences online.

With the ease that these platforms provided, sharing experiences over the internet soon became more attractive to the average person. People began spending less time connecting in the real world and more time on their phones or other electronic devices. Currently, social media platforms have billions of daily active users! Each spending several hours a day on these websites.

1998 **2020**

This is why most companies decided to move their advertisements from physical billboards, television, and radio ads to social media sites, where over a billion users spend hours browsing online every day.

But why do people spend so much time on these platforms? Because social media sites allow any user to create content with nothing more than a phone and access to the internet. Users can find like-minded individuals or even content that suit their own preferences. From funny videos to adorable cats, the options are limitless for creators to make and for audiences to enjoy.

This is where our social media marketer comes into the picture. These professionals help big companies and small businesses to best present their products or services across various social media platforms.

In this way, our marketer can help companies not only make videos or pictures that will catch a viewer's attention but also target the right type of audience that will be more likely to buy their product or service.

The marketer's job is far from done though. They must also keep an eye on their advertisements by watching their metrics to make sure they are engaging the right customers.
facebook
Order Now!
Monthly Sales
Profit Records
Daily Signups
Spent on Ads
75%
65%
April

On Facebook, companies can display products in news feeds while putting easy links for users to purchase from.

On YouTube, creators can make videos about items they want to sell, further convincing audiences by showing live demos of the product's quality.

On TikTok, companies can make short video clips and challenges, which can potentially go viral if enough users join the trend!

On Instagram, companies can present beautiful pictures and easy links to customers who may see exactly what they're looking for.

On Twitter, companies can sneak in a brief explanation of their offers to catch the attention of busy individuals on the platform.

But now that you know what a Social Media Marketer does, it's important to know how they got to that position.

There is always the traditional route of going to school, obtaining a degree in digital marketing, and then finding the right company to work for after graduation.

Another route is to join a boot camp that can teach you the fundamentals of a Social Media Marketer. This is a great way to figure out the basics and switch careers at any age!

You can also learn these concepts on your own. Many videos, tutorials, books, and courses are offered by large social media platforms. All of which allow you to study at your own pace.

When applying for a job as a Social Media Marketer, it's important to be able to show your work and how you are able to create specialised strategies and concepts for clients.

The best way to show your work is often with a marketing portfolio. This is normally a website where you can introduce yourself and show off your previous projects so that companies can see your marketing skills.

After finding a job though, your work has only begun. As a marketer, you'll need to keep up to date with what marketing trends are currently popular and which ones are becoming outdated.

This is why it's important for you to remain creative and always try to think outside of the box. That way, your work stays fresh and ahead of the curve!

But now it's up to you to decide if this is the right career path to embark upon. Remember that every job requires skill, and every skill requires practice to consistently improve. And as long as you have passion, you'll have the right attitude it takes to thrive.

Shubhi Saxena
Founder, Unibino

My Inspiration

As a parent in this ever-changing world, it can sometimes feel overwhelming when it comes to our children's futures. New technologies seem to be arising almost every day, and with so many innovations, it creates unique professions which many of us wouldn't have dreamed to be necessary only a few years ago. Which to me is a good thing. Because with so much variety, my children can have the opportunity to pick a career that will fit their personalities and build upon their strengths. As you may imagine, this desire within me to provide my children with the resources they needed to thrive, led me to search out books that would be easy enough for them to understand while teaching them about various professions.

Only, I found that these books were few and far between. Even if I could find a book about a certain profession geared towards young readers, I found them sparse inside and limited to only certain careers that may not fit my children's abilities. This is when I came up with the idea to write my own children's books, teaching them about all the various careers in the modern world. After months of researching different professions and learning more than I ever expected, I quickly realised this was going to be a bigger project than I first anticipated. I dove into the histories of these professions, discovering links to the past, and why these professions were now so important.

Ultimately my goal was to offer my children options, to show them that there is no one set path for everyone. But in this, I stumbled upon something bigger. I wanted to share this with future generations. To share with all children and parents about these careers, to help spark curiosity, and to instil a passion for the future. Everyone has special talents and abilities, and I hope that this series will be able to offer clarity and inspiration to children around the world. Because at the end of the day, it's never too early to start dreaming and never too late to take action. With this, I hope you enjoy this series and that your young ones become the best versions of themselves as they can achieve.

www.ingramcontent.com/pod-product-compliance
Ingram Content Group UK Ltd.
Pitfield, Milton Keynes, MK11 3LW, UK
UKHW060102300726
14090UKWH00003B/348

* 9 7 8 9 8 1 1 8 6 0 7 1 3 *